# THANK GOD I'M NOT FAMOUS

# THANK GOD I'M NOT FAMOUS

## THE LIFE OF CHRISTIAN CHARLES ROBERTS

## MY BOOK OF MAGIC MOMENTS

## BY CHRISTIAN CHARLES ROBERTS

StoryTerrace®

Dedicated to my grandchildren: Elektra Lily, Neon Luca and Echo Honor so they will know who their Grumpy was.

**Text** Christian Charles Roberts with Clara Salaman

**Design** Grade Design and Adeline Media, London

**Copyright** © Christian Charles Roberts and Story Terrace

**Cover photo** © Heather-Dawn Scott

**Text is private and confidential**

First print November 2016

Story Terrace·

www.StoryTerrace.com

# CONTENTS

PROLOGUE     9

1. GROWING UP AND DRESSING UP     13
(1946-1963)

2. CHRISTIAN THE FILM STAR     25
(1964-1974)

3. CHRISTIAN THE THEATRE ACTOR     49
(1974-1980)

4. CHRISTIAN THE MILKMAN     57
(1980-1987)

5. CHRISTIAN THE ENTREPRENEUR     63
(1988-1995)

6. CHRISTIAN THE RESTAURATEUR     71
(1997-2014)

# PROLOGUE

*"This, above all: to thine own self be true,*
*And it must follow, as the night the day,*
*Thou canst not then be false to any man."*

*William Shakespeare*

A day in the life of a self-confessed hedonist. Barbados, Year 2008.

*(Written for* The Sunday Times Magazine *series 'A Life in the Day' but never published)*

I awake around 8.30am to the sound of waves breaking on the shore. I stagger downstairs for some coffee and Greek yoghurt with honey, which I consume in front of my computer whilst checking my emails. Now is the time for my first cigar of the day. I like Montechristo Puritos. Mild and so much better than cigarettes.

Three days of the week, at 10am, I go to the gym for a one hour workout with my personal trainer, Dirty Diana. She really puts me through it so that I feel I can relax for the rest of the day. On the other two days I go riding on my beautiful paint horse, Jack. We meander through the cane fields and gullies that tourists would be lucky to see.

After all this strenuous exercise I take a short swim followed by a shower and a shave. On weekends I spend part of my mornings on my lilo, anchored to a buoy in the bay for one hour, maximum: my total exposure to the sun for the week.

Lunch is always at 1pm when I repair to the restaurant for a couple of rum sours and a cigar before eating. Lunch is usually a discussion over sausage and mash with my restaurant manager, Rory Rodger, as to how things are going. A bottle of rosé will pass our lips before a Bajan coffee and another cigar to finish things off. I then return home, next door, for a siesta until 6.30pm.

*The restaurant is situated within five metres of the beach. All the tables have a sea view and turtles have been known to lay their eggs there in full view of the dining customers. The sand on the beach comes and goes a bit with the seasons but remains pretty much the same. This has not changed in the 11 years that we have been open. I like to be in the restaurant for 7.30pm to receive the guests. I have an excellent staff, many of whom have been with me since our opening in 1997. I tell them they are all in show business. We have a large celebrity clientele whose privacy I respect, although I might add I do have Simon Cowell's authorisation to trumpet his comment that the Lone Star is "probably the best restaurant in the world!"*

*If I am dining with friends I will most likely have a vodka martini followed by a fillet steak and a bottle of Chateau Clarke. After dinner, a couple of Bajan coffees and big cigars and then I'm off to bed at about 11pm. I watch some TV — Inspector Morse is my favourite — and I am sound asleep by midnight. On Sunday nights, I head to Holetown to watch the transvestites perform at Ragamuffins, hosted by my friends Nuru Patterson and Crystal Clarke, followed by a spot of karaoke.*

It is now 2016 and on rereading this article recently I realised what an indolent life I had been leading. I am now 72 and in June 2015 I collapsed and was rushed into hospital where I had a complicated operation to remove my colon. After six months in hospital I was discharged to my home. I now have a colostomy bag and

I feed myself liquid via a tube. I have no taste whatsoever and alcohol gives me no pleasure. My only pleasures now are the memories I have. My years of hedonism have caught up with me.

Who was this person I had become? I thought that perhaps I should look back and try to find out what had happened and whether I had always been this way. So I shall start at the very beginning.

# 1

## GROWING UP AND DRESSING UP

My great-grandparents on my father's side, Louisa Barber and Edward Roberts, moved from Wales in 1870 to take over a dairy in Teddington, Middlesex. When Edward died, Louisa married one of her employees, Handel Alfred Job (pronounced Jobe) and they changed the name of the dairy to HA Job Ltd or Job's Dairy. My father, Douglas, was to take over this family business, as was my brother after him. My maternal great-grandmother was also a formidable woman — she too was called Louisa — Louisa Florentina Hedwig Joskey. She was born in Germany in 1855 and moved to England to marry my great-grandfather, Charles Albert Beard.

I was born on the day of the air attack on Monte Cassino, March 17th, 1944, which also makes me a Pisces, a Monkey in Chinese astrology, and in Numerology the dates give me 'double creativity and confidence' (a cocky actor?). I was

*Douglas Roberts*

*Portrait of my grandfather, HA Roberts*

*My great-grandmother, Louisa Barber*

born at Court Close near Abingdon in Berkshire and my sister
Susan (eight years older than me) always tells the story of
being made a fuss of by the American soldiers at the time
of my birth. My father was by now managing director of the
dairy, which had an important role in the war effort. He had
moved my mother Betty, my sister Susan and my brother
Simon here as soon as he could from Walton-on-Thames. In
1948, the year of my sister Patricia's birth, my father bought
a 50-acre farm called Long Orchard in Cobham for £13,000.
My brother Simon still lives there.

I attended St Maur's convent school. The nuns were a
little frightening but I much admired their theatricality — the
costumes, the religious services, the reverent tones. I remember asking a nun, "Why am I who I am?" An early hint at
personality problems, perhaps, but the nuns certainly ignited
a love of dressing up, much encouraged by my wonderful,
loving mother who would painstakingly stitch up my costumes. I'd spend hours playing with my friends — we devised
great games of pirates and cowboys, or sometimes Napoleonic
soldiers. My grandfather, also known as the Guvn'r (CEO of
the dairy) was a great influence on my love of showbusiness;
to my delight he would take me to pantomimes and the circus
where I was once lucky enough to see Coco the Clown. Some-
where amongst all this I had my tonsils taken out and was put
in a girl's ward as they read my name as Christine. But most
memorably for me, I appeared in my first school play — the
Nativity — in which they gave me a choice of part: a shepherd

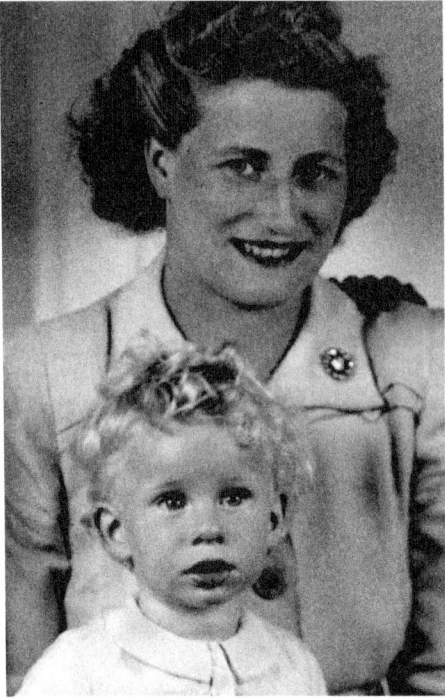

*Me with my mother in 1946*

*My great-grandfather, with my great-great-grandmother*

expressing awe at the baby Jesus or a King with no line count. I chose the King — he had a far superior costume.

My other grandfather, Walter Hazard Webb, known as Whoopee, and my grandmother, Gaggy, lived in a cottage in the grounds. He was a lovely upright man, tall and slim with Brylcreemed hair. He would take the train into London every day and do something important in the City. He was an inveterate smoker and asked that a packet of Woodbines and a box of Swan Vestas be buried with him. My grandfather, HA Roberts, my father, my uncle and my brother had all gone to Cranleigh School in Surrey. I sat the entrance exams and

*Portrait of my mother, Betty Roberts*

fortunately passed but unfortunately missed my first few days of school as I had the 'flu. A boy called Patrick Gilpin was assigned to look after me. He was to become a lifelong friend.

We had a very talented music teacher at Cranleigh, Dr Philip Wilkinson, who decided that I could sing and he gave me invaluable lessons in how to produce my voice. I sang a song in the music competition: 'The Trout', I think, by Schubert. I didn't win. However, soon I did begin to achieve: I became a soloist in the choir, singing 'Early One Morning' at the school concert, and to cap it all I gained the Leaping Wolf badge in Cubs (not to be underrated). I also got into the rugby team which was to become a lifelong passion. I remember playing my first real acting role, I was Abraham in *Romeo and Juliet,* produced by the wonderful Bunny Green who was to become my singing teacher over the next few years and taught me a great deal about voice production. My chief line was, "Do you bite your thumb at us, sir?" I never quite understood what it meant but over the years I have often said lines that were quite incomprehensible to me.

What's more: I thrashed Puddick in the boxing competition.

At the age of 12, I was cast in my first major role — Frederick in *Pirates of Penzance,* directed by an audacious new master called Lance Marshall who decided to stage Marlowe's *Tamburlaine* which had not been produced anywhere in over 50 years. I played Mycetes and now knew for certain that I loved acting. And then the next year the school play was

*My grandfather in the choir at Cranleigh*

*Dr Faustus*, another Christopher Marlowe, which was a fantastic opportunity for me with lines I remember to this day. "Was this the face that launched a thousand ships?" and, "Her lips suck forth my soul," whilst attempting to kiss a pretty fourth form boy. My friend Graham Patterson's father came to see this. His name was Val Parnell and he was a huge producer in TV at the time, the Simon Cowell of his day. He told me that he thought I should pursue a career in acting. I didn't forget it. He had planted a belief.

Meanwhile, I thrashed Sharman in boxing.

In 1958 I fell in love with Shakespeare, via Judi Dench's

*Me in the choir*

breasts. My grandfather had taken me to see *A Midsummer Night's Dream* at the Old Vic, a play that was always to stay with me. I took Shakespeare to heart and back to school with me: I won the elocution competition with my rendition of the prologue to *Henry V*, "Oh for a muse of fire... " (after a glass too many I still bore my friends with it to this day). My grandfather then took me to see another production of the 'Dream at Regent's Park open air theatre. But I missed Judi Dench's bosoms. It just wasn't quite the same. Not long later my wonderful grandfather died, not knowing what world he had opened up to me. I owe him so much. He would have been pleased to see me play Oberon in the next school production where we even brought in girls from the local girl's school. Not quite sure what he would have made of the amount of time I spent backstage holding the hand of Joan Shenton (my Titania). I was developing a keen interest in girls; my only previous crush had been on a boy called Lionel Daury on a holiday in the South of France.

I turned 16 at the beginning of the 1960s and my interest in acting and the opposite sex continued. I decorated the cellar at Long Orchard as a nightclub and had a great party. I danced the night away with Susie Thompson whilst Fats Domino sang 'Blueberry Hill'. My love of music had been nurtured during the Asian 'flu epidemic when I went to stay with a friend to recuperate, as my own parents were away on holiday. I watched a lot of TV at his house and started my record collection, my first purchase being 'Stupid Cupid' by

Connie Francis, shortly followed by Elvis. That summer, I
went to stay with friends in Canada, where I took a shine to a
girl called Linda Hissink. We sat in the back row of the movies
kissing and cuddling, one eye on the film, of course — Sandra
Dee in *A Summer Place*, as I recall.

I scraped through my A-levels, with a pass in History and
English — I was very good at the 'quoting' parts but I hated
exams and swore I'd never take another one (I've kept my
oath). That summer whilst holidaying in the South of France
with my family, I met a man who was to have a great influence on me. He ran the hotel we were staying at, the Tour de
L'Esquillon, and his name was Sebastian de Robert. He was
a wonderful host and I noticed the way he always had interesting chats with his guests; this was the year of the student
riots in Paris and he took great pains to explain it all to me.
I was later to try and emulate his behaviour when running my
own establishment.

My father never really approved of me wanting to be
an actor. He didn't consider it a 'proper job'. He would have
much preferred that I worked in his industry, the dairy. He
was a very traditional guy but had a great heart. He looked
after his employees with great care: he was one of the first
employers to secure a pension scheme for his workers and
even took them away on annual holidays, something again I
was later to attempt to emulate. It was Christmas time in 1963
and I started dating the daughter of a friend of my father's.
However, shortly afterwards she dumped me and I found

myself crying on her sister's shoulder, so to speak. Pattie was a lovely girl. It was a particularly bad winter and I'd only just learnt to drive so didn't want to drive Pattie home in bad conditions so asked if she could stay the night at Long Orchard. As luck wouldn't have it, in the middle of the night my father received a telephone call from her 'boyfriend' and came to find me. He stumbled across the pair of us in bed together. He was most upset and summoned me to his room for a dressing down. "The worst thing is," he said, "I'm playing golf with her father tomorrow." I think my poor father was a bit stuck with what to do with me at this stage.

The whole family went on a cruise to South Africa (where I was keen to talk to as many people as I could about apartheid, but it wasn't easy at that time). On the way back my father met a man whose son was off to study French at Grenoble University and he decided that that was exactly what his son should do too.

So I found myself a cheap apartment in Grenoble and enrolled at the university, but I'm afraid I didn't attend many classes and learnt most of my French in the bars and restaurants. I met a lovely French girl called Joelle and she moved in with me. We found a fabulous restaurant where we could have a three-course meal and a litre of wine for ten francs. The barman was from St Tropez and he invited us down there to stay with his parents. I was driving a Triumph Vitesse convertible at the time, which was quite a fast car (I blame the car) and I crashed it driving down to St Tropez. No one was hurt and we chugged on into the town where I had it repaired. St Tropez was at the height of Brigitte Bardot mania at the time and I felt very hip being there.

When we returned to Grenoble I discovered that my old flame Susie Thompson was there; she was now going out with Denny Cordell Laverack, who was an old school friend of mine who had played Bottom in *A Midsummers Night's Dream* when I played Oberon. He had just had an interesting time: he'd been in a club in Paris where Chet Baker, the jazz trumpeter, was playing. Chet was on the skids and Denny offered to be his manager. Chet agreed! Denny dropped the Laverack on his name and went on to have a huge career in the music business. He went on to produce the Moody Blues hit 'Go Now', and discovered Joe Cocker and the Cranberries. We all went to Paris and had a great time; I went to a bullfight, which I loved, having myself enjoyed the great British blood sport of foxhunting and having been bloodied myself (not forgetting the thrashings I gave Puddick and Sharman). It all felt very Hemingway, very 60s, very happening. But it was time for me to take my own bull by the horns and pursue the things I wanted to pursue.

# 2

## CHRISTIAN THE FILM STAR

In 1964 I got in to the Royal Academy of Dramatic Art, having auditioned with the aid of Renu Setna, an Indian actor and friend of a friend. He coached me through the rejection of Falstaff's speech from *Henry V*.

I was 19 years old and I hadn't realised what a privileged life I had led up until then. I was completely unprepared for the diversity of people I was to meet in my class at RADA, people of all ages and backgrounds from diverse countries. There was a group of us who were all about the same age and became good friends: Kenneth Cranham, Richard Winter (Warwick), Tony Maylam, Roger Lloyd Pack and Angela Schoular. Richard and I and a friend from Cranleigh moved into a flat in Tufnell Park and my girlfriend at the time, Sue Paisley, would come and stay.

The day at RADA started at 10am with classes in movement, speech, singing and fencing. Regional accents were not in vogue (not that I had one) and 'Standard English'

*Tom Chadbon*
*(part of 'the in crowd')*

*Ken Cranham*
*(part of 'the in crowd')*

*Richard Warwick*
*(part of 'the in crowd')*

*Roger Lloyd-Pack*
*(part of 'the in crowd')*

was taught. In the afternoons we'd rehearse plays for our tests. Each term there would be two tests, one Modern and one Shakespeare. We had a wonderful voice teacher, Clifford Turner, who had worked with King George VI to help rid him of his stutter (later immortalised in *The King's Speech*). I remember he told me "You have charm, boy. Use it!" In the holidays we would sometimes do outside productions which students volunteered to be in. We performed *Julius Caesar* on the steps of the Imperial War Museum. As a first termer I had the tiny part of Cicero but it was a great experience working alongside more senior students.

That first summer, Richard (Rick), Ken Cranham and I took off to Salou in Spain, smoking joints all the way down. We were unsure of where the Spanish border was but were pretty sure we must have passed it and lit up another great bloody joint, only to see the border guards approaching. In those days it was seven years in jail for marijuana. We shoved the joint down the back of the seat and somehow, though searching the boot, they missed it.

Back at RADA, as well as performing myself, I went to see a phenomenal amount of theatre and music shows: Ray Charles, *Beyond the Fringe* (Peter Cook, Dudley Moore, Jonathan Miller and Alan Bennett), The Supremes at Hammersmith and Peter O'Toole playing Hamlet. Later I saw *Dr Faustus* starring Elizabeth Taylor and Richard Burton (how I envied him), met Noel Coward backstage after his last ever role in *A Suite in Three Keys*, and Fats Domino (with a support act with sound problems who got booed off the stage: The Bee Gees). Years later I saw Bob Marley and the Wailers do their first ever London gig. I was like a sponge. I drove down to the first ever Glastonbury festival — it was called Shepton Mallet back then. Mind you, I have no idea who was playing — we spent most of the time off our heads in a tent. But I'm getting ahead of myself.

The Vanburgh was RADA's showcase theatre where critics, agents and the general public would come to watch us. My first major role was the part of Dunois (clad in hard-to-manoeuvre armour) in George Bernard Shaw's *St Joan*. An important show for me as my old pal, Graham Parnell, came to see it with his step father, Val Parnell, who was now working for the theatrical agent Roy Mosely. He arranged for me to go for a meeting with Roy, who signed me up.

Six weeks after leaving RADA, Roy sent me along for an audition with the casting director Harvey Woods who was casting a film, based on a true story, called *To Sir, With Love*, to be directed by James Clavell (author of *Shogun*). It was a great part, Denham, and was second billing to the Oscar-winning Sidney Poitier. I was incredibly nervous when I read for it. However, at the recall, Clavell introduced me to Lulu — who was already a huge star — saying, 'Christian, meet Lulu. You will be working together!' I rang my parents straight away! They were going to pay me £75 a week — a phenomenal amount of money at the time. My mother was thrilled but my father was not overly

*Poster for To Sir, With Love*

impressed; he thought it a ridiculous amount of money considering his milkmen were on £1,000 a year.

We started filming at the end of May, 1966. Sidney Poitier was a wonderful gentleman in the true sense of the word. He would encourage and help all of us; an exceptionally generous actor. It was to be a bumper year for him: he also went on to film *In the Heat of the Night* and *Guess Who's Coming to Dinner*, and all three films were groundbreaking in terms of race at the time.

I fell for my co-star Judy Geeson and we went everywhere together, head over heels in love. Anyone who was anyone at that time hung out at Alvaro's in the King's Road, Chelsea —

the Rolling Stones, Michael Caine, Roman Polanski; it was the place to be and be seen (which very much mattered to me at the time; one night I'd take Lulu there and the next Judy, very much enjoying playing the role of the 'film star'.) I was to learn a lot about hosting an establishment from Johnny Gold who ran Dolly's nightclub in Jermyn Street (and later, Tramps) where we would dance the night away, often joined by Sidney Poitier himself! It was July now and Judy and I watched the infamous World Cup Final at James Clavell's house. Life could not get any better!

After filming Judy continued her on-off relationship with her French boyfriend with whom I felt I just couldn't compete; yet to my surprise, she seemed rather pissed off when I had a brief holiday affair with a French girl. Judy came out and met me in Paris and our relationship became official.

*To Sir with Love* cost Columbia Pictures $600,000 and within its first year had netted $14 million. This was despite them delaying its release as they were worried about the American market understanding our cockney accents; however, when it was eventually released in the States it opened to rave reviews which netted me a five-year contract with Columbia. I was loaned out to Hammer and made my second feature film, *The Anniversary*, which had been a play in London. Only now the role of 'Mum' was to be taken by the legendary Bette Davis. She was a real 'grande dame'. To the actors she was fine because she knew she needed them to react to her, but to everyone else she was unpleasant with a massive ego. She

*Still from To Sir, With Love, starring Sidney Poitier*

didn't like the director, Alvin Rakoff, and after two weeks on set she refused to turn up unless he was replaced. "He's making me move for the camera instead of it moving for me." This was my first experience of the power of a Hollywood film star. Rakoff was duly given the elbow and in came the old-school director Roy Baker, who would do Ms Davis' bidding. My part was that of the cheeky youngest son who often had a nice one-liner to end the scenes. Ms Davis didn't like this and soon put a stop to any potential scene-stealing from me, making sure that all my best lines were cut. "Miss Davis does not feel this line would be appropriate... " the director would tell me. I was cowed into submission and have regretted it ever

*Starring in The Anniversary with Bette Davis*

*Poster for The Anniversary*

since. However, I must add, I am eternally grateful to Bette Davis for providing a highlight in my mother's life: the three of us had lunch together and Ms Davis was charm personified.

My next Columbia picture was called *The Desperados*. It was a Western. I couldn't believe it; I loved Westerns. Although the film was to be shot in Spain, they sent me out to America to learn to ride Western style with Ralph McCutcheon, a legend in Hollywood who had trained Champion the Wonder Horse and had worked with all the great cowboys: Roy Rogers, Gene Autrey and Tex Ritter. Although I was already a very proficient rider, it was a fantastic experience learning how to leap into the saddle and neck rein the horse in true cowboy fashion. It being the summer of love, I detoured via San Francisco where I heard some cool bands with my mate Ian Whitcomb who had had a smash hit in the American Top Ten called 'You Really Turn Me On'.

Filming for *The Desperados* began in March in Madrid. It was directed by Henry Levin and starred Jack Palance (I was playing his son), Vince Edwards, George Maharis, Neville Brand, Sylvia Syms and Kate O'Mara. Neville Brand had been a highly decorated World War II hero, but unfortunately was now a total drunk. Every morning my taxi would pick him up at 6am whereupon he would appear with a bottle of vodka in his hand and would be halfway through it by the time we got to the set. Needless to say, he was a liability to work with. On set he would have to have numerous vitamin B12 injections in his arse throughout the day to keep him halfway

*Poster for The Desperados*

sober. One night, I got into a bit of an argument with him in a nightclub in Madrid. The next day, Jack Palance, who was a real gentleman and had begun to treat me like a real son, made him apologise to me. Jack wore tweed suits and smoked a pipe; he was quite an anglophile. I thought he was great.

But not as great as Kate O'Mara: I fell for her (Judy and I had on-ed and off-ed and petered out but remain friends to this day). Kate and I began an affair. She had quite a wildcat reputation but she was always a pussycat to me. After filming I accompanied her (she was already quite a star) to the Cannes film festival and swanned about with her — nobody had any idea who I was. After meeting the director's wife, Hilda Gilbert, at a dinner party, Kate and I went to Rome to audition for a Harold Robbins film, *The Adventurers*, about a South American playboy and his two buddies. I was quite cocky in those days and felt the audition had gone well — I was up for buddy number one. I got the part but Kate didn't get hers.

I'd bought myself a 1954 Bentley 'R type' for £500 and had it sprayed white at Job's dairy with my father's blessing and then drove down to Rome for the filming. The director, Lewis Gilbert, was impressed with the car and used it in the film — Candice Bergen can be seen driving it into the piazza for her wedding. I'd been put up in a beautiful little hotel down by the beach called Hotel Corsetti. Also staying there were Peter Cook and Dudley Moore, my heroes! Dudley was going out with Suzy Kendall who had been in *To Sir, With Love* with me. Life continued to be hugely exciting. I was on

$400-a-week expenses (an almighty sum in those days) and us three 'adventurers', Bekin Feamu, Tommy Bergen and myself, had a wonderful time in Rome. On Sundays all the cast would come down to the beach hotel and visit me. I had a Super-8 camera and spent a lot of time filming us all, on and off set. Olivia de Havilland was in the film and the role of my father was played by Rossano Brazzi, who I must thank profusely for my mother's next highlight: she had come out to visit me and the three of us dined together. He charmed her completely.

The last of the filming was in LA. Roy Mosely came out to see me and promote me. I went to various auditions, one of which was at MGM's Culver City where we heard that Elvis Presley was filming *Change of Habit*. We walked in, as bold as brass, and there was Elvis in a white suit, seated at a piano, in between takes. I remember he was tinkling away *My Melancholy Baby*. When he finished we went up to him and started to chat. He was so friendly, telling us he desperately wanted to perform in England but that the Colonel (Parker) wouldn't let him. He signed a still for me.

When *The Adventurers* was released my parents accompanied me to the screening in Leicester Square. "Far too much sex," was my father's only comment. It was a bit of a miserable evening. The film turned out to be a flop; however, I still believe it was rather underrated.

At this time an old friend of mine from prep school and RADA, Tony Maylam, was doing a pilot for an American show called *The Dating Game*. He asked me to do the show but I was turned down as a date by Pat Booth. The show went on to be a success with Cilla Black as *Blind Date*!

My third Columbia picture was called *The Mind of Mr Soames* starring Terence Stamp, a man emerging from a lifetime of being in a coma. It was directed by Alan Clarke and was his first foray into film. I think I was miscast: Alan was having difficulty getting the performance he wanted out of me and eventually told me he was going to dub my part. Everything had gone so right for me up until this point and I was very depressed at this failure. None of my LA auditions had proved fruitful.

Back in Blighty, I had a good time hanging out with my old

*Starring in The Adventurers with Charles Aznavour*

RADA friends and got myself involved in rugby again, playing for the Old Cranleighans where I discovered that I was surprisingly fit. I spent a lot of time with a beautiful woman, Salvador Dali's muse, whose name was Amanda Lear and who had allegedly had a sex change. She had a deep, sexy voice much like Marlene Dietrich. Rick, Amanda and I used to spend a lot of time together, going to the pictures (Greta Garbo movies) and going out to dinner.

I then made a TV movie for Universal Studios, *The Berlin Affair*, which was to be shot in Berlin and directed by David Lowell-Rich. Both the director and I developed a crush on Pascale Petit, a beautiful French actress a few years my senior.

*The Dating Game with Tony Maylam and Pat Booth*

*Me with Pascale*

I turned out to be the lucky one and we began our very own Berlin affair. She and I were staying in the same hotel and we enjoyed both it and the city to the max. Our relationship lasted two years; I am a terrible hoarder and still have love letters from her.

My next film was called *The Last Valley*, directed by James Clavell who was giving me a second bite of the cherry after *To Sir*, and was filmed out in Innsbruck, Austria. It was set during the Hundred Years War and a medieval village had been constructed in a valley in the mountains. The film starred Omar Sharif and Michael Caine. We'd walk into places and the bands would start playing the *Dr Zhivago* theme tune, and Michael

Caine would pretend to be pissed off. I remember that Pascale came out to visit me and it turned out she knew Mr Sharif; I was rather jealous because in the film he steals my girl. In the evenings we'd play poker with our peculiar Austrian money, Mr Sharif gently refraining saying he didn't want to fleece us. My parents came out onto the set and met him. I remember how appalled my father was whilst out on location; "All these people sitting around doing nothing."

Back in England, I missed out on a few jobs I desperately wanted. I met Bob Fosse and had three screen tests for *Cabaret* and was thoroughly disappointed to lose out to Michael York (he was a bit hotter than I was at the time). I really wanted to play Prince Rupert in *Cromwell*, but my fellow RADA colleague, Timothy Dalton, got that one! *The Mind of Mr Soames* opened to poor reviews. *The Last Valley* opened to good reviews but it didn't do well at the box office. Things weren't working out quite as I had hoped. Then I got myself arrested whilst turning up to a music gig at a college in Roehampton in my Bentley; the police were at the gate and thought I was a drug dealer. They took me off to Putney police station and took my prints and searched my car, in which they found some traces of marijuana in the back ashtrays. They took me to court where my lawyer successfully argued that the drugs could not possibly have been mine as I was in the front seat at the time of arrest.

Pascale and I were still seeing each other, despite the fact she was living in Paris. My next project was to be directed

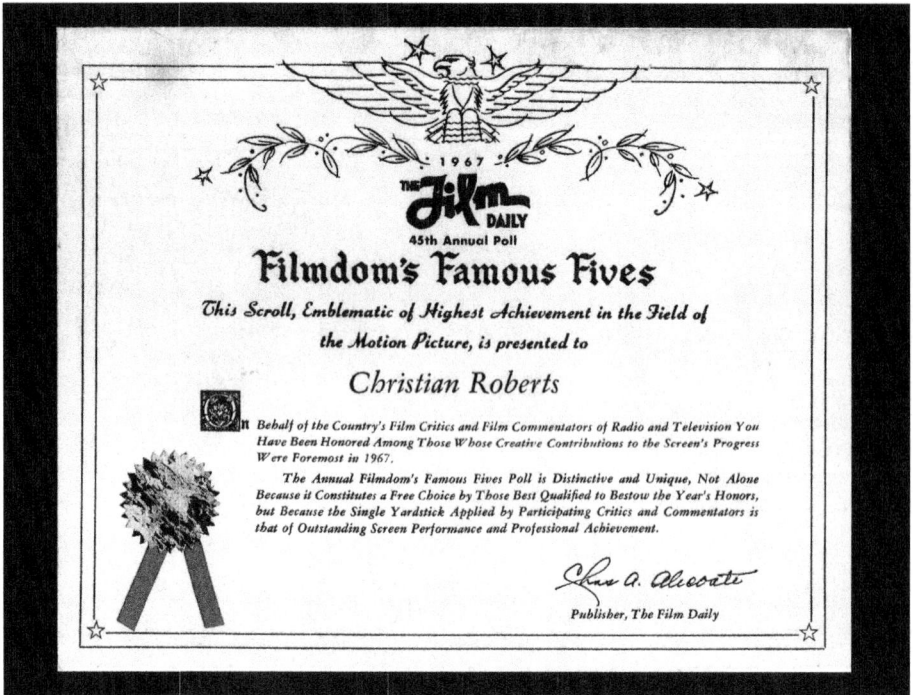

*Award from the Filmdom's Famous Fives*

by the comedy genius Michael Mills. It was called *Clochemerle*, and I was playing the part of Hippolyte. It was filmed in Villefranche in France. I saw Pascale as much as I could, and then in the August I went to Paris to stay in her apartment but stupidly invited my friends Ken and Rick to join us. We were smoking a lot of dope and in the end she had just had enough of us; she thought I was being an idiot, wasting my life. She ended the relationship. I was devastated. Us three boys drove onwards but Rick and Ken went back for work reasons. Acting had gone a bit quiet for me; I found myself alone in Spain and called my old friend Judy Geeson who came out to join me. Then Amanda Lear asked us to join her in Cadoques where

*International Laurel Award*

she was posing for Salvador Dali. So we visited her in his studio where he was painting her, and the four of us went out for dinner; here he asked me whether I would send him some flowers from Harrods that were made from fabric in exchange for one of his paintings. On my return I went to Harrods and bought the flowers and sent them out to him. I never heard a word. I was hoping for at least a signed letter.

In the early '70s I was being invited to quite a few film premieres as a result of my Columbia contract. In November of 1970 I got tickets to see the premiere of *Waterloo* with Rod Steiger and Christopher Plummer. I decided to take my young nephew and godson Andrew to see the film with me. He was only eight years old at the time. I like to think that the film made a lasting impression on him as he has now gone on to be a hugely successful historian. One of his works is *Napoleon the Great*, a bestseller.

The last film I made was shot in Tenerife. It was called *Timanfaya* (Mountain of Fire) and I was the lead. I've never seen it, but I would like to as I did my own stunts, one of which involved being shot at the summit of the aforementioned mountain and tumbling all the way down to my death. Whilst flying to Lanzarote for another scene, I met a Swedish air hostess called Sylvie and we struck up a relationship.

*Poster for Timanfaya*

Roy and I had a push on my career and flew out to LA to do the rounds, but it wasn't until I was back in London that I had an epiphany. I was talking to the daughter of a friend of mine who was studying at the Acting Studio; she was so full of enthusiasm and passion for acting which I think led to the epiphany. I was fed up with hanging around Hollywood trying to be a film star. I had always wanted to be an actor but I wasn't practising my craft.

Back in the UK, my love life took an interesting turn. Sylvie and I were not really working out. I was being hit on by a girlfriend of my old school friend, Hugh Smallwood. She was an American called Carole Grey. In fact, the night before her wedding to Hugh, she came knocking on my door under some pretence. I did not take her up on it. Unsurprisingly, their honeymoon was a disaster, not helped by most of Hugh's mates turning up as a surprise. She left her own honeymoon and instead ended up going to the island of Skiathos with Hugh's flatmate, Christine Carswell. On her return to London, once more she came a-knocking, this time bringing Christine along as 'gooseberry'. After they left I realised that I was incredibly attracted to the gooseberry.

This was 1973. Christine and I began seeing each other. She was a receptionist at Andre Bernard, the hairdressers in Mount Street and would go on to do the accounts of all three branches. It wasn't for a while that I began to realise what an incredible person she was, and how deeply I was falling in love with her. Clearly, she was beautiful (just before I met her she had been runner-up in Cosmopolitan's Supergirl Contest), but I hadn't yet discovered how special she was. That happened during a trip we made to Turkey in my Land Rover which I had converted, fixing a couple of bunk beds in the back. I had invested my Job's Dairy shares, £25,000, in a Western film to be shot in Southern Turkey. We had several adventures on the way there, including being woken up by soldiers and being awoken by a fierce herdsman with a shotgun for whom, out of politeness, I found myself swallowing a sheep's eye to make him happy. We spent a happy night in the Istanbul Hilton drinking champagne in the bath, after which

## OUR SEARCH FOR A COSMO SUPERGIRL GOES ON

Pretty, aren't they? The girls pictured here, we mean. Perhaps your friends say you are prettier . . . if so, these are the pages you can't afford to skip. Last month we launched our *1973 Cosmo Supergirl Contest* to find the prettiest, best dressed, most *alive* girls around. Wella, the largest international hair company in the world, are helping us in our search—you'll see the Cosmo Supergirl poster in most hairdressers. This must be the most exciting contest ever—the first prize includes a trip round the world by BOAC.
Much more than a model girl contest, this is the search to find the girl with something extra —a mind of her own. Do you fill the bill? Then fill in the coupon below and send a good clear picture of yourself *today!* To whet your appetite, here are the prizes: a round-the-world trip via Frankfurt, Tokyo, Sydney, Honolulu and New York as Wella's guest, staying at luxury hotels; £200 worth of clothes from the International Wool Secretariat; a diamond ring designed by Ernest Blyth and Frances Beck, value £150; an amazing Zandra Rhodes dress; Estée Lauder cosmetics, value £50; a set of luggage from Condotti; a year's hair care from

*Christine in Cosmopolitan*

Christine had to return for work. By this stage I had seen what a beautiful person Christine was: she was sincere and practical and very self-effacing, which I really liked. When I got home I proposed to her. Initially she laughed in my face and said I was drunk, which I probably was, but eventually I managed to persuade her that I was serious. Meanwhile things were not going well on the set with the film. Terry York, a British stuntman, was having a nightmare of a time with the Turkish horses; the Turks treat their animals appallingly and he couldn't find a decent horse to train. But worse was to come: the entire film set was then washed away (with my

*Me with Christine in St Tropez, 1992*

money) in a freak storm. I was devastated. Christine and I had to return to pick up the Land Rover, which was hung over the back of a boat to transport it to Rhodes. We decided to stay in Rhodes for a few days before going on to Italy. We found a little pension in a white-washed village called Lindos where we thought we would have a fuss-free little wedding. I had a gold band made up, but unfortunately the van was robbed and the band disappeared. In the end we had a low-key wedding in Barnes Registry Office on 26th September with just our parents in attendance. Afterwards, back at Hugh's flat, about 40 friends turned up to celebrate. We bought a little house in the Farnham area called Sunnyside, thanks to some help from my father. And then, most strangely, my father gave me a theatre connection: a colleague at the dairy was on the board of Farnham Theatre. I met up with him and was introduced to Ian Mullins, the director of the Castle Theatre, who happened to be a massive Bette Davis fan! I was in there! At last I would begin my acting training in earnest!

# 3

## CHRISTIAN THE
## THEATRE ACTOR

I was extremely nervous at my first audition; I hadn't done any theatre since my RADA days. Graham Berown was directing *A Flea in her Ear* by George Feydeau. He could tell I was very nervous and tried to help me with some exercises in relaxation. He said he would let me know. He did. They wanted me. I was to be in repertory theatre: performing the same play in the evening for three weeks whilst rehearsing other plays in the daytime. I was overjoyed. My salary would be £23 per week. A long way off from my film star rates but I was delighted.

The Castle was closing, and a new theatre, the Redgrave Theatre, was being built in honour of Michael Redgrave who lived nearby. The opening production was to be *Romeo and Juliet*, in which I was to play Paris. There was to be a special gala show to kick it all off in front of Princess Margaret and Lord Snowdon. Some 'serious' theatre actors were brought in for this show: William Gaunt, Anna Wing, Edward Jewesbury, John Sterland and Carolyn Lister. I learnt so much just from watching them rehearse and was gradually becoming much more confident with stage work. Perhaps a little too confident. During the royal performance, once I'd fought my duel and been fatally wounded, I was meant to lie dead on the stage until the end of the play; however, it had been a long tech and dress run the night before, and unfortunately I nodded off and woke with a start during Romeo's most moving moments. I sat bolt upright, quickly realised where I was and fell back down dead again. Princess Margaret kindly sympathised with me after the show; she said, "I was feeling a little dozy at that stage too."

Then, a short while later, lo and behold, I was to play the part I had lost out on to Michael York. Bill Gaunt was to direct *Cabaret*. He brought in Zoe Wannamaker to play the part of Sally Bowles. I loved the part of Cliff and loved the singing but hated having to drink a raw egg every night. The next show was *Royal Hunt of the Sun* followed by *The Devil's Disciple* and then the world premiere of William Douglas-Home's play *The Lord's Lieutenant*, the music for which was being written, on my recommendation by Ian Whitcomb. I had to play the guitar and sing. The show attracted London critics, most of whom savaged it, except for Harold Hobson, importantly, who loved it. I performed in a string of plays at the Redgrave Theatre and was incredibly happy there, especially as Christine was now working in the restaurant. We put on: *The National Health*, by Peter Nicholls, *The Rivals* by Sheridan, *Move Over Mrs*

*Starring as a '70s pop star in* The Lord's Lieutenant

*Markham, Ten Little Niggers* (politically incorrect, I know, but that's how it was called back then) and *Arsenic and Old Lace*. I began to feel like I was really learning my craft now. My first really classical role was Trofimov in *The Cherry Orchard*, which was a daunting task, but Ian Mullins brought in a wonderful actress called Jospehine Tewson to play Madame Ranevsky. She was very generous in helping me.

Ian called me in to his office and suggested I spread my acting wings elsewhere. I saw his point: I had become very comfortable at Farnham and, although disappointed, I agreed that I needed new challenges. But then someone dropped out of his next production, a Noel Coward anthology, and he offered me a part. I already knew all the words and had met the 'master'. I leapt at it and had a wonderful time; many was the night I had to help out a lovely but drunken actor, Gerald Flood. During the finale, the entire cast at the front of the stage were meant to individually sing the lines to 'Let's Do It', but alas, for Gerald, the mixture of doing it and alcohol proved confusing. Then came another unexpected call from Redgrave Theatre, this time from Graham Berowne who was directing *The Gentle Hook*.

During all this our beautiful daughter Lucy was born on 26th February 1976, in Cambridge Military Hospital in Aldershot. We named her Lucinda which means 'bringer of light'.

I did then take up Ian's suggestion and began to spread my wings. I went to Salisbury Playhouse to do Alan Ayckbourne's *Absurd Person Singular* and the musical *Tarantara! Tarantara!* Then I went up to the Theatre Royal in York to do the Scottish play, directed by David Thacker, starring John Rhys-Davies and Alison Fiske. I played Lennox. Also in the cast in his first job, as an ASM and minor part, was a young boy called Pierce Brosnan; God knows what happened to him...

Meanwhile we were trying to mount a production of a play called *Ostrich* in the West End with the writer Martin Donovan, but the money kept falling through and Graham Berowne had had enough of procrastinations and lack of funds, so a new director, Philip Morgan, came on board. Whilst the problems with *Ostrich* continued, Philip suggested we re-

*Performing in Macbeth, which also featured a then unknown Pierce Brosnan*

hearse Strindberg's *The Creditors* at the Three Horseshoes pub in Hampstead. However, the other actors weren't happy that *Ostrich* was not happening in the West End as promised, and the production fell apart. I also did a new musical at Watford Palace Theatre called *Foxy* (not a success) before signing for yet another season at the Redgrave!

I went straight into rehearsals for *Spider's Web* by Agatha Christie, then the musical *Salad Days*. This was followed by *The Importance of Being Earnest* (we had a wonderful Lady Bracknell, Mary Griffiths) at the same time as performing *Travesties;* the two plays were not dissimilar and occasionally a line or two slipped from one production into the other. Lastly, another Alan Ayckebourne, *Time and Time Again.*

Around this time Chris Masters and I started a lunchtime theatre at the Bellerby Theatre in Guildford, sponsored by my brother's company Southern Fast Food (which sold Kentucky Fried Chicken and had an outlet in Guildford). We put on *The Peter Pan Man,* in which I played JM Barrie and Helen Simnett played Peter Pan. We followed this with *A Slight Accident* by James Saunders. Amongst all this, I managed to fit in my first ever television jobs: *Blake's 7* with my old RADA chum Gareth Thomas, and a show called *Secret Army.*

Meanwhile, in 1978, our second child Benjamin Henry Roberts had been born (Benjamin after Christine's father and Henry after mine). I remember his christening; when the priest walked in, Lucy asked in a loud voice, "Is that God?" We moved into The Cottage at Headley Fields in Hampshire.

I was feeling a little daunted about how I was going to support a growing family on an actor's salary. Then something happened that was to change the course of my life. I was attending the Job's Long Service Dinner, as I tried to do every year, and something about the speeches moved me more than they ever had before. My father had started this dinner a long time ago. He treated his employees with such dignity, something I was later to try to emulate; some of them were like members of the family. Stan Harris had worked for my father for 40 years, formerly as a lorry driver and latterly as my father's chauffeur, and had recently died after a long illness. He had looked after the horses and lived in a caravan next to the stables. He

*Lucy and Ben*

meant an awful lot to me; he had taught me to ride as a boy and had been a witness at our wedding. As I listened, I made the decision there and then that I had finished with acting: I had done what I had set out to do with it and I had had a very good run. It was time for me to work at the dairy. I went straight over to my brother and informed him of this. He told me to come and see him at the office the next day, which I did. My father was there and they wanted to know how serious I was, my brother pointing out that I would have to turn up on time. I was aghast; "What do you think I have had to do in the theatre all these years? The curtain doesn't wait for actors." They told me I would have to start at the bottom. I didn't mind. It was an easy decision. My father was really happy: at last — a proper job!

I did one more play at the Redgrave and a TV series called *Feet First* (again, not a success). I finished the series on the 28th of January and started as a milkman on the 29th.

# 4

## CHRISTIAN THE MILKMAN

So, Sean Connery started life as a milkman and became a film star. Well, I did it the other way around: I had been a film star and became a milkman. I perceived it as a challenging new role. Job's Dairy was a very successful business, had been going since the 1860s and employed over a thousand people. Now they had a thousand and one. My brother Simon had worked out a training programme for me: I was to spend my first week in Tiny Howard's office. Tiny was a huge man and had been a director of Job's since the war; he had been my Uncle Alan's chief engineer when he had been a bomber pilot in the RAF, and after the war my Uncle had offered him a job. Tiny was in charge of all technical aspects of the production of milk at the Dairy. The milk would arrive from the farms in large sterilised tankers from which it was pumped into the pasteurising machines, then bottled, crated and loaded onto lorries to take to the distribution depots. I spent a thoroughly fascinating week with him, reading books about milk production and listening to many dairy anecdotes. Tiny liked a drink and the office bar would open at midday.

My second week was spent in the laboratory with Miss Macintosh, testing samples of milk from the farms as well as at every other stage of the production process. Simon had also arranged for me to go on a course at the Institute of Directors in London. This was a business course dealing with balance sheets and profit and loss accounts. I returned the next day to work on the reception bank; this was where the milk came in from the farms. Large pipes had to be attached to the tankers to pump the milk into the huge silos in the dairy. After the milk had been pumped out, other pumps were then attached to wash out and sterilise the tankers. I worked there merrily for two weeks, thinking I knew what I was doing, before disaster struck. Some of the tankers had two compartments; I had emptied out one and then put on the pumps to wash it out without emptying out the second compartment, ruining hundreds of gallons of milk. Normally this would have been a sacking offence; instead I got a humiliating telling-off. I then spent the whole of March on the Process Floor where the milk was pasteurised, then moved onto the block pack cartonning machine, then the Cream Room, and then the Filling Room where the milk went into bottles. I ended up on the Despatch Bank hauling the stacks of full milk crates onto the lorries before moving on to the Engineer's Department and a week with each of the deputy dairy directors learning about costings and general staff management. At the end of April I finished up in the Transport Department where all the lorries were serviced and where all the milk floats were looked after, and the Body Repair Shop (Job's built a lot of its vehicles and this was where it was done). There was no department I didn't work in. My brother then put me on another course on the financing side of things at the Institute of Directors.

Every year Job's held its annual Sports Day at the London Irish Rugby Ground in Shepperton. It was always a great day; all the branches of the Dairy competed against each other and the highlight was a tug of war. My father always gave a speech. He was quite a performer himself.

Training over, I was ready to start my milk rounds. My first round was at Goring. I went out with an experienced rounds-man to learn the ropes. I had to get up at 3am to get to work for 4am. We had 500 customers on that round and all transactions had to be logged into the book. We would collect the money on Fridays or Saturdays, and woe betide you if your book was either 'over' or 'short'. It was a beautiful summer and once I got over the early rises it was a joy to be out in the open air. Then in the September I started work at Basingstoke. Being one of the largest branches, there were 30 rounds. After that I worked at Tadley, then did stints at Tilehurst, Shinfield, Woodley, Ashford, Sunbury, Hanworth, Hampton, Hounslow, Croydon and Tolworth, and went on another intensive financial course.

It was 1980 now and it was being proposed, for the first time since the dairy had begun, that we drop down to a six-day week (instead of seven) which would involve logistical problems of extra milk storage. After careful planning the operation was successful, and Job's secured a deal with Sainsbury's and Marks and Spencer supplying them with cartonned milk. My brother was a great business man; the days of fast food were in their infancy, but he saw the potential, and because of this Job's Dairy had two lucrative sidelines. He had met Colonel Sanders in Kentucky in the 1960s and secured the franchise of some 50 Kentucky Fried Chicken outlets in the south of England, from Margate to Plymouth. Job's also supplied all goods that fast-food businesses needed. This time, to complete my experiences in the family business, Simon put me on the shop floor of a Kentucky Fried Chicken shop before appointing me as Health and Safety Director for Job's. That year I sat on the top table at the Long Service Dinner.

In January 1981, we moved house to a place in Odiham in Hampshire. I was now on a good salary, and happily married with two children. I worked all week at my 'proper job' and on Saturdays I played rugby for the Old Cranleighans; I was captain of the extra 'A' XVs. Simon then organised for me to go to the States to a dairy in Boston, Wingate Dairy, where they gave me some more training. I was most impressed with their frozen cakes and, with Simon's backing, invested in *Freezeflow* — a cake you take and eat straight out of the freezer. It didn't work. Now that my training was completed,

Simon let me go off to do a lunchtime play at Bellerby for a few weeks called *Bird Bath,* which we took to Salisbury for a few more weeks. Meanwhile Job's was expanding into property with investments in Australia; he sent me out there to look at them. Christine and I had a wonderful trip, crossing the date line twice on my birthday!

Then in 1986, my father died from a type of leukaemia. My mother was bereft without him, broken hearted; their marriage had been a very happy one. My sister's son had been training at a military academy in the north of England and they took my mother along to watch the passing out ceremony. She appeared to nod off during it. However, when they

*The family in 1981, at my parents' ruby wedding anniversary*

tried to wake her, she had gone. It was only six months since my father had died. And then the following year, my brother, with great foresight as usual, saw what was happening in the dairy business (the collapse of doorstep delivery and the rise of supermarkets) and sold Job's to Unigate. We still had 50 Kentucky Fried Chicken shops.

However, I was now without a job.

# 5

## CHRISTIAN THE ENTREPRENEUR

I went back to what I knew: the theatre. Yet by this stage in my life, I had accumulated many more skills (and a nice house with a swimming pool called 'Highcroft'). I put out my tentacles and began by doing a bit of acting again. I performed in a play in Basingstoke called *Having a Ball* from which came my next job: *Noises Off* at the Redgrave where I played the director. The real director was a man called Bob Carlton, who used to run Bubble Theatre. I got to know him very well. The first play I did for him was *From a Jack to a King*, a rock-and-roll version of Macbeth which he had written and which we performed on his barge in Regent's Park. He then told me all about a production he had written, after seeing the film *Forbidden Planet* (based on *The Tempest*) for Bubble Theatre. His version was full of rock-and-roll music and was called *Return of the Forbidden Planet*. This excited me greatly. I said I would raise the money to put it on in the West End.

*In Highcroft with my family, 1985*

That December, we did a rock-and-roll version of *Romeo and Juliet* and performed it in my house. I invited a lot of wealthy friends to invest. We took it up to Edinburgh where we performed *From a Jack to a King* in the evenings and *Romeo and Juliet* in the street in the day (it was only 20 minutes long). I remember driving the van dressed as a vicar and the police treating me most respectfully. Most of the people in *Romeo and Juliet* went on to be in *Forbidden Planet*.

My next job was at the Belgrade in Coventry doing *The Unexpected Guest* where Bob came to visit me. We got talking to the artistic director who loved the sound of *Return*

*From a Jack to a King, in the West End*

*of the Forbiddden Planet* and said we could open it there in the April. We now had a deadline. We got the show on and I invited all sorts of wealthy people. The evening went fantastically and we raised over £600,000. A West End producer, Andre Ptazinski, wanted to take the show on as co-producer. So Bob and myself formed a company with all the actors (pretty avant-garde at the time). We called ourselves Rhythm Method Productions and we had 50% of the shares whilst Andre had the other 50. I had learnt an awful lot about business by now and was confident setting up a business and doing percentages. I was also playing Dr Prospero, which I loved.

*Return of the Forbidden Planet* opened at the Cambridge Theatre in the September. It attained reasonable reviews but was not good enough to go beyond Christmas unless we achieved more sales. A couple of weeks before we were due to close, a roaming actor critic from the Gloria Hunniford TV show *Sunday Sunday* was sent off to review random West End shows. Well, to our incredible fortune, this guy came to see *Forbidden Planet* and he absolutely loved it and raved about it on Gloria's show. Well, the next day the box office telephone didn't stop ringing and the show just took off. I have to say that it was one of the happiest times of my life. They'd bring the figures to me in my dressing room every night; we broke the record at the time for the longest-running show at the Cambridge with over 2,000 performances.

It was an incredible show; all the actors were musical, most of them played instruments, and we were all very happy to be sharing the profits. There was a great unity in the cast. Then in the January I started to lose my voice. I went to see a specialist and was diagnosed with tuberculosis for which the doctor put me on some very heavy antibiotics. We did a version of the show for the Children's Royal Variety Show, and then we performed at the Olivier Awards where we won Best Musical of the Year and were handed the award by Petula Clark (we were up against *Miss Saigon* and didn't think we stood a chance). We performed 'Great Balls of Fire!' Bob was terribly embarrassed to get the award; he was a real theatre man, not in it for the glory.

*Poster for Return to the Forbidden Planet*

*Award nomination for Return to the Forbidden Planet*

So after two years of performing eight shows a week at the Cambridge, I came out of it in 1991. Christine and I flew on Concorde to Barbados for a holiday. I fell in love with the place and couldn't quite get it out of my head. On my return, Bob and I continued with Rhythm Method and put on *From a Jack to a King* at the Ambassador's Theatre. It was not the huge success that *Forbidden Planet* was. We had made a big mistake: we sold it as 'sex and drugs and rock-and-roll' which foolishly eliminates half your audience: children. Family outings were a write off. Meanwhile, *Forbidden Planet* opened off Broadway but the Americans didn't really get it.

*The sign that inspired the name of my restaurant: the Lone Star*

Around this time, I met someone who was to become one of my very best friends, the legendary Pattie Boyd (she of 'Something' and 'Layla' fame). We are twins, sharing the same birth year, date and entrance time to this world. We try to celebrate our birthday together every year, and one year went to Dublin for St Patrick's Day. She is a super woman and a very talented photographer.

My brother then sold the franchises of Kentucky Fried Chicken, so I had money to invest and was ready for a new challenge. I returned to Barbados where I stumbled across a disused garage on a beach with a peeling paint sign, which read 'Lone Star'. This was to be my next project: I was going to build a beautiful house. Mike Pemberton and a friend, Steve Cox (owner of Prego restaurant in London), suggested turning it into a restaurant.

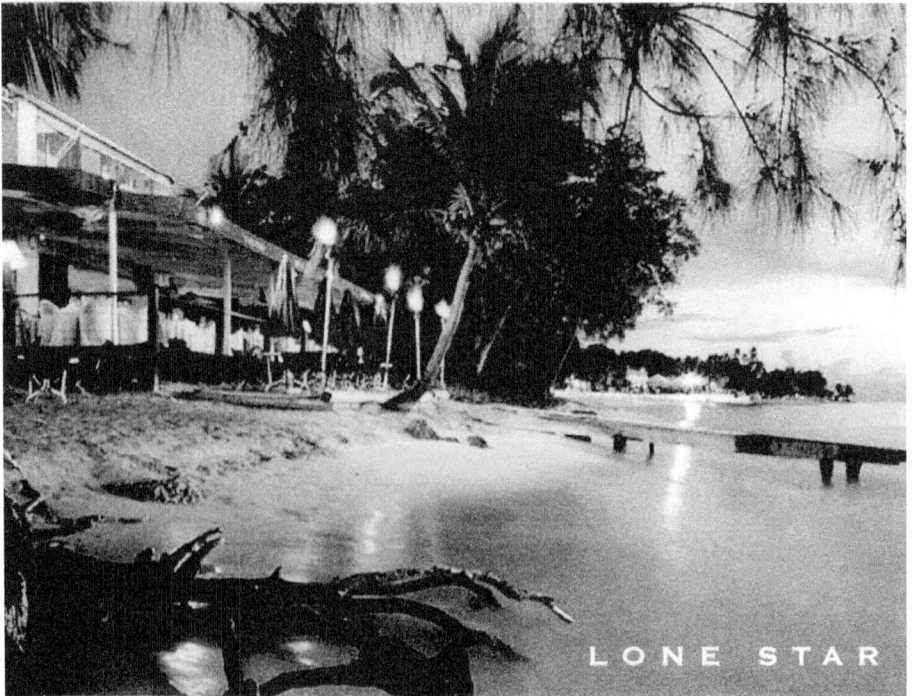

*Booklet for the Lone Star restaurant, Barbados*

# 6

## CHRISTIAN THE RESTAURATEUR

In 1997 I opened the Lone Star restaurant. It had taken three years to renovate, to do up the house and get the restaurant into shape. There were three other investors; I had a 50% stake, whilst the other 50 was jointly owned by Mike Pemberton, Steve Cox and Eddie Fairless. Steve Cox brought over the chef from Prego. In the running of the business I took inspiration from the way my father had run his and set up an award scheme: a badge after one year's service, another after five years and another after 10. I'd also take the staff on cruises to other islands.

These were very happy years and the Lone Star did really well; pretty soon it was running itself. It seated over 250 customers and the place was always buzzing. I had some wonderful people working with me, many of whom I am still friends with to this day. I bought my beloved horse, Jack, and went riding every day. I even bought a racehorse, Passionaria, which won a few races. I loved being a host and

*My beloved horse, Jack*

being able to use my performing skills on a daily basis. I used to go to Ragamuffins on a Sunday night to see the transvestites perform. Nuru Patterson who worked there came to join me at the Lone Star as one of my managers. I also helped Crystal Clarke, who worked at Ragamuffins, to open her own rum shop called O'Cristals. It was successful but sadly burnt down in March 2007.

One particularly pleasant memory comes to mind. For many years our rugby club had been setting up a fund; we pooled the money and 75 of us went on a cruise on the *QE2* around the Caribbean to celebrate the millennium. Then on New Year's Eve 1999 we all piled into the Lone Star for a

*La Tour de L'Esquillon — my inspiration for the Lone Star*

BBQ lunch.

Two less pleasant things happened during these years. I remember receiving a devastating phone call from my daughter Lucy in which she told me that she was addicted to drugs. It was awful, just awful. Christine and I went out to visit her in a clinic in Arizona. She was to go through rehab four more times before getting herself together (I have immense admiration for her; not long ago she graduated from Edinburgh with an MA in psychology and has now chosen to bring up a child alone. Meanwhile Ben has had two kids, Neon and Elektra, so we have three gorgeous grandchildren now). The other unpleasant thing that happened during those years was that Mike Pemberton and I fell out. In addition, Simon Cox started doing things to the restaurant without consulting me; thus our relationships began falling apart. In the end I bought the others out and it was only then that I really began to enjoy running the show.

The Lone Star became a real celebrity hang out: a stream of the rich and famous would come and dine there, from Cilla Black to Harry Belafonte. Michael Caine turned up once and said "You ain't done too bad, 'ave you, Christian." Michael Winner called the Lone Star "The Ivy of the Caribbean". So, yes, it was indeed a hedonistic time; but I worked hard for

*A sunny day at the Lone Star*

*Above: Portrait of a barmaid at Lone Star. Credit: Heather-Dawn Scott. Below: A Bar at the Folies-Bergère, by Édouard Manet*

my hedonism, and upon reflection I can see that it has been a lifetime of preparing myself for that ultimate role of 'host'.

Then in 2013, after many glorious years, I sold the Lone Star. Over the years, people had kept making me offers but then Mr JJB Sports, Dave Whealan, made an offer that I simply couldn't refuse. Besides, I wanted to hand down a legacy to my children and grandchildren. So that was the end of the Lone Star, indisputably my proudest venture in life, after my marriage. I miss the Lone Star, I miss the people and am still in touch with a lot of them. My manager Rory went on to take on a beach bar, Little Bristol in Speightstown, which I have invested in.

Christine had always preferred London to Barbados and I came back to join her in our flat in Knightsbridge; yet with one foot still in Barbados, partly because of the slow bureaucracy there and partly because I permanently rent a place there, have money in the beach bar and had a very important reason to return there in October this year.

My love affair with Shakespeare and the Caribbean continues. I recently produced a film: *A Caribbean Dream* (based on *A Midsummer Night's Dream*) shot in Barbados and written by a Barbadian, Shakirah M. Bourne, which screened in October; I was due to play Theseus but it turned out that life had other plans.

The morning after Patti's wedding, a year ago, I remember feeling a little odd when I awoke. But nothing prepared me for what was coming. The last thing I remember is being in

*Nuru Patterson, Jason Hydeman and Rory Rodger on a staff outing*

the hall of our flat in Knightsbridge, and then the next thing I know I am in hospital and they've whipped out my colon and my stomach. Apparently I had a colon infection. From that moment on, my world as I knew it was turned upside down. I am now fed through a tube and excrete through a bag. I cannot eat and alcohol tastes wrong. Smoking is the only pleasure I have left. I suppose I am paying for the life I have lived; my capacity for pleasure has at last been thwarted, and those hedonistic days of the Lone Star seem a long way off. But I can safely say, on reflection, that I haven't done too badly in my life, as Michael Caine so rightly put it. I have always found pleasure in my work, whether it be as a film star, a grafting theatre actor, a milkman, a business man or a restaurateur; I have grasped the opportunities that have come my way. One thing has always led to another, right from the beginning when my grandfather first took me to see Shakespeare.

I am NOT famous, thank God, and in this day and age I am glad I am not. I still have my privacy.

I don't doubt for a moment that things happen for a reason. If there are lessons to be learned from this life I would say: go with the flow. Oh, and try to take people as they are until you know any better.

*Our revels now are ended. These our actors,*
*As I foretold you, were all spirits and*
*Are melted into air, into thin air:*
*And, like the baseless fabric of this vision,*
*The cloud-capp'd towers, the gorgeous palaces,*
*The solemn temples, the great globe itself,*
*Ye all which it inherit, shall dissolve*
*And, like this insubstantial pageant faded,*
*Leave not a rack behind. We are such stuff*
*As dreams are made on, and our little life*
*Is rounded with a sleep.*
*William Shakespeare — from* The Tempest, *Act IV, Scene 1*

*Poster for Caribbean Dream, a film I co-produced in Barbados in 2015*

*Christine and me in Turkey, 1991*

Printed in Great Britain
by Amazon